REV. GABRIEL WHITLOCK

THE UNTOLD STORY OF ST. PHILIP NERI

The Saint Who Laughed His Way to Holiness!

Copyright © 2024 by Rev. Gabriel Whitlock

All rights reserved. No part of this publication may be reproduced, stored or transmitted in any form or by any means, electronic, mechanical, photocopying, recording, scanning, or otherwise without written permission from the publisher. It is illegal to copy this book, post it to a website, or distribute it by any other means without permission.

First edition

This book was professionally typeset on Reedsy.
Find out more at reedsy.com

Contents

Preface	v
1 THE EARLY YEARS OF A JOYFUL SOUL	1
Neri's Childhood and Youth	1
A Call to the Priesthood	3
The Impact of His Family	4
The Development of His Character	6
2 THE ORATORIAN WAY OF LIFE	8
The Founding of the Oratory	8
The Oratory's Unique Approach to Spirituality	10
The Role of Community	11
The Practice of Contemplation	11
The Oratory's Impact on Rome	12
Spiritual Renewal	12
Social Reform	13
Cultural Influence	13
The Oratory Spreads Throughout Europe	14
The Early Years	14
The Oratory's Impact	15
The Oratory Today	15
3 NERI'S EXTRAORDINARY GIFTS	17
The Gift of Laughter and Joy	17
The Gift of Healing and Miracles	18
The Gift of Discernment And Wisdom	19
The Gift of Prophecy and Vision	21
4 NERI'S RELATIONSHIP WITH THE CHURCH	23
Devotion to The Pope	23

	Role in Church Reforms	24
	Influence on Counter-Reformation	25
	Legacy Within The Church	27
5	NERI'S SPIRITUAL TEACHINGS	29
	The Importance of Joy and Laughter	29
	The Practice of Simplicity and Humility	30
	The Role of Community and Fellowship	32
	The Path of Spiritual Growth	33
6	NERI'S IMPACT ON SOCIETY	35
	Care for the Poor and Needy	35
	Promoting Education and Culture	36
	Influence on Art and Literature	37
	Legacy of Rome and Beyond	38
7	NERI'S DEATH AND LEGACY	40
	The Circumstances of His Death	40
	The Canonization Process	41
	The Spread of His Devotion	42
	The Effect of His Life on the World	44
8	ST. PHILIP NERI TODAY	46
	The Relevance of His Teachings	46
	Oratory in the Modern World	48
	The Devotion to St. Philip Neri	50
	The Saint Who Continues To Inspire	51
9	CONCLUSION	53
	The Enduring Legacy of St. Philip Neri	53

Preface

Few Catholic saints are as mysterious, appealing, or inspiring as Saint Philip Neri. Neri, known as the "Apostle of Rome," lived a life full of pleasure, purity, and a deep love for God and humanity. Nonetheless, despite his enormous influence on the church and the world, his narrative is mostly unknown, a hidden gem waiting to be uncovered.

Neri's existence was a conundrum. He was born in Florence, Italy, around 1515, the son of a lowly tailor. However, his spirit was far from ordinary. From a young age, he showed an extraordinary capacity for joy, with a contagious laugh that seemed to light up every room he visited. This seemingly contradictory characteristic, along with a strong spirituality, would become the defining feature of his life and career.

As a young man, Neri felt a strong pull to the priesthood. He joined the Oratory of Saint John the Baptist in Rome, a community of secular clerics committed to spiritual reform. His infectious energy and charming demeanor immediately attracted others in. Recognizing his ability, his superiors urged him to engage in more active ministry.

Neri's true vocation would emerge during the turbulent sixteenth century in Rome. The city was in a state of spiritual and social upheaval, beset by corruption, religious indifference, and a growing feeling of moral degradation. Neri, with his unshakeable faith and great optimism, was determined to restore the church in the heart of the Eternal City.

In 1551, Neri founded a new society called the Oratory of Divine Love. Unlike traditional religious orders, the oratory was a lay community that welcomed both clergy and laypeople. Its members were bound together by a common desire for spiritual growth, intellectual advancement, and charitable service. Neri's Oratory immediately became a place of spiritual rebirth, attracting people from all walks of life.

Neri's ministry was distinguished by its unique combination of spirituality and practicality. He was an expert storyteller who used comedy, tales, and plain language to express profound spiritual truths. He was also an extremely hard worker, spending countless hours visiting the sick, the impoverished, and the disenfranchised. His kindness and generosity were legendary, and he was renowned for his ability to offer joy and hope to even the most despondent people.

Neri's life was characterized by a sequence of remarkable incidents and mystical encounters. He was famous for his miraculous healings, prophetic visions, and ability to read the minds and intents of others. However, he always maintained that these abilities were not his own but rather manifestations of God's love acting through him.

Neri died quietly in Rome in 1595, the culmination of a life of dedication and sacrifice. He was canonized by Pope Gregory XV in 1622, and his feast day is May 26. Today, Saint Philip Neri is revered as the patron saint of Rome, comedians, and everyone seeking a pleasant and full spiritual existence.

This book tries to reveal the unseen narrative of Saint Philip Neri, a man who defied expectations, inspired countless people, and left an enduring legacy that still resonates today. It's a narrative about joy, holiness, and the transformational power of love. Neri's life teaches us important lessons about the value of faith, optimism, and a sense of humor in our own spiritual journeys.

One

THE EARLY YEARS OF A JOYFUL SOUL

Neri's Childhood and Youth

Philip Neri was born on December 21, 1515, in the thriving city of Florence, Italy. His parents, Tommaso and Lucrezia Neri, were modest people who lived a simple existence in the city center. Neri was the second of five children, raised in a close-knit family that instilled in him a strong faith and compassion for others.

As a toddler, Neri had a wonderful capacity for joy and laughter. His contagious smile and fun nature delighted his family and friends. He had a genuine curiosity about the world around him and was always eager to discover and learn.

Neri's early education was conducted in Florence. He went to a local grammar school and obtained rudimentary education in Latin, grammar, and rhetoric. However, his primary passion was in the spiritual sphere. He was captivated by the beauty and mystery of the Catholic faith, and he spent a lot of his leisure time reading religious books and attending church services.

As a teen, Neri had a deep spiritual awakening. One day, while praying in a church, he sensed a strong presence of God surrounding him. This encounter gave him a sense of calm and purpose, and it strengthened his resolve to devote his life to God's service.

Neri's parents were supportive of his spiritual goals. They urged him to pursue a religious vocation and even offered to assist him with the financial costs of theology education. With their permission, Neri left Florence and headed to Rome, the heart of the Catholic Church.

In Rome, Neri joined the Oratory of Saint John the Baptist, a group of secular clergy dedicated to spiritual reform. There, he completed his theology studies and gained a better understanding of the faith. He also began to work on his preaching talents, developing his ability to communicate spiritual truths in a clear and engaging manner.

Neri spent his early years in Saint John the Baptist's Oratory. He learned from seasoned spiritual directors and became acquainted with the city's vibrant intellectual and spiritual culture. He also began to feel a great affection for the church and a strong devotion to its purpose.

After finishing his studies, Neri was consecrated a priest in 1551. He continued to serve at Saint John the Baptist's Oratory, but he also expanded his ministry by preaching, teaching, and caring for the impoverished and sick. His contagious energy and captivating demeanor drew others to him, and he quickly became a popular figure in the Roman community.

A Call to the Priesthood

Neri's upbringing and youth were characterized by a strong sense of faith and love for God. This spiritual basis eventually led him to pursue a priestly vocation, a path that would forever alter his life and the lives of countless others.

Neri's early religious experiences were influenced by his family. His parents, Tommaso and Lucrezia, were devoted Catholics who fostered in their children an appreciation for the Church and its traditions. Neri was particularly captivated by the beauty and mystery of the Mass, and he frequently spent hours in prayer and reflection.

As a teenager, Neri developed a strong desire to serve God. He felt a tremendous pull to the priesthood, as if he were being drawn to a greater cause. This calling was not always simple to understand or express, but it was a driving force in his life.

Neri's decision to become a priest was impacted by several things. One of the most crucial was his strong devotion to the Church. He saw the church as Christ's body and was deeply committed to its goal of spreading the gospel and bringing salvation to the world.

Another crucial component was Neri's desire to help people. He has a caring heart and was always willing to assist those in need. He believed that the priesthood provided him with a unique chance to serve God and his people in a meaningful way.

Neri's parents supported his decision to become a priest. They recognized his deep faith and dedication to serve God, and they encouraged him to pursue his calling. With their permission, Neri left Florence and headed to Rome, the heart of the Catholic Church.

In Rome, Neri joined the Oratory of Saint John the Baptist, a group of secular clergy dedicated to spiritual reform. There, he completed his theology studies and gained a better understanding of the faith. He also began to work on his preaching talents, developing his ability to communicate spiritual truths in a clear and engaging manner.

Neri spent his early years in Saint John the Baptist's Oratory. He learned from seasoned spiritual directors and became acquainted with the city's vibrant intellectual and spiritual culture. He also began to feel a great affection for the church and a strong devotion to its purpose.

After finishing his studies, Neri was consecrated a priest in 1551. He continued to serve at Saint John the Baptist's Oratory, but he also expanded his ministry by preaching, teaching, and caring for the impoverished and sick. His contagious energy and captivating demeanor drew others to him, and he quickly became a popular figure in the Roman community.

The Impact of His Family

Neri's childhood and development were heavily influenced by his family. His parents, Tommaso and Lucrezia, were devoted Catholics who fostered in their children an appreciation for the Church and its traditions. This solid spiritual basis would play an important part in Neri's life, directing him toward a priestly vocation and driving him to serve God and his people.

Neri's family surrounded him with love and support. He was the second of five children raised in a close-knit household that emphasized faith, hard work, and compassion. His parents were always there to support him, providing encouragement, direction, and unconditional love.

Neri's father, Tommaso, was a tailor by profession. He worked long hours to support his family, instilling in his children a strong work ethic. Tommaso was also a fervent Catholic, and he instilled his faith in his children by example and education.

Lucrezia, Neri's mother, was a lovely and caring woman. She was highly devout, and she spent a lot of time praying and caring for her family. Lucrezia had a significant impact on Neri's spiritual development, encouraging him to pursue his call to the priesthood.

Neri's siblings played an important influence in his life. He had three brothers and one sister, and they were all close to one another. Neri's siblings offered him friendship, encouragement, and a sense of belonging.

Neri's family encountered a number of difficulties during his upbringing. At one point, his father lost his job, and the family struggled to get by. Despite these challenges, Neri's family remained together and resilient. They relied on their religion to get them through difficult circumstances, and they emerged stronger than ever.

Neri's family's experiences had a significant impact on his personality. He learned the value of tenacity, resilience, and compassion. He also developed a great appreciation for the blessings in his life.

Neri's family was a source of strength and inspiration throughout his life. Even after leaving Florence to follow his religious calling, he remained close to his family. He paid them visits as much as possible and wrote to them on a regular basis.

Neri's family was an important aspect of his life. They raised him in a loving and supportive environment, established in him a strong faith, and assisted him in developing the character attributes that would serve him well in his priestly profession.

The Development of His Character

Neri's childhood and youth were heavily influenced by his family, his experiences, and his spiritual growth. These formative years helped shape his character, which is a unique blend of joy, compassion, humility, and steadfast faith.

One of the most striking elements of Neri's personality was his infectious enthusiasm. He had a natural desire to laugh and be happy since he was a child. He seemed to enjoy everything he did, and his good attitude was contagious. Neri's pleasure was more than just a surface quality; it was anchored in his strong faith and love for God. He thought that God was the source of all goodness and happiness, and he strived to embody that joy in his life.

Neri's joy was also intimately related to his sense of humor. He had a gift for telling stories, and he frequently used humor to convey spiritual truths. His laughter and jokes were more than just a source of amusement; they were a method to connect with others and spread joy.

Another important feature of Neri's personality was his kindness. He had a strong empathy for people and was always willing to assist those in need. He was especially concerned about the impoverished and oppressed, and he devoted a lot of his time and energy to helping them.

Neri's compassion was based on his faith. He felt that all people were formed in God's image and treated them with decency and respect. He perceived others' suffering as a reflection of his own failings, and he was driven to alleviate it as a method of serving God.

Neri was also a person of profound humility. He was never one to brag about his successes or spiritual achievements. Instead, he was always ready to recognize his own limitations and give God credit for everything he had accomplished.

Neri's humility was directly tied to his faith. He believed that true greatness came from serving others rather than achieving personal success. He was always willing to step back and let others take credit.

Neri's character was shaped by both his experiences and his spiritual development. Despite a variety of hardships throughout his childhood and youth, he never lost faith or hope. These events helped him cultivate resilience, tenacity, and a strong feeling of gratitude.

Neri's spiritual development also had a significant impact on his character. He spent most of his time in prayer and thought, striving to live his life in line with God's will. His faith provided him a sense of purpose and direction, and it assisted him in developing the virtues that would be useful in his priesthood.

Neri's personality was a unique and amazing combination of enthusiasm, compassion, humility, and steadfast faith. These characteristics would benefit him throughout his life and continue to inspire people long after he died.

Two

THE ORATORIAN WAY OF LIFE

The Founding of the Oratory

Saint Philip Neri created the Oratory of Divine Love in Rome in 1551, and it is a unique lay community dedicated to spiritual rejuvenation and service. The Oratory's origins can be traced back to Neri's personal journey and the spiritual climate of 16th-century Rome.

Neri was born in Florence, Italy, in 1515. As a young man, he felt a strong call to the priesthood and enrolled in the Oratory of Saint John the Baptist, Rome. There, he acquired a strong devotion to the church and a desire to serve God and his people.

However, Neri was dissatisfied with the usual monastic existence. He saw a need for a more adaptable kind of religious life that would allow him to reach out to a broader spectrum of individuals. He also believed that the church needed to be reformed and renewed, and he was determined to participate in that process.

THE ORATORIAN WAY OF LIFE

Neri left Saint John the Baptist's Oratory in 1548 to pursue a more autonomous life. He spent his time praying, researching, and serving the underprivileged. He also began to assemble a small circle of friends who were captivated by his captivating demeanor and profound spirituality.

Neri's concept for a new lay community developed over time. He intended to build a place where people might gather to pray, study, and serve God in a more casual and easygoing setting. He also intended to promote the value of joy, laughter, and a good attitude toward life.

In 1551, Neri and his friends founded the Oratory of Divine Love in a small room near the Church of San Girolamo della Carità. The Oratory swiftly gained prominence, attracting visitors from all walks of life.

The Oratory's approach to spirituality was unique in its day. It highlighted the value of community, camaraderie, and shared experiences. Members of the Oratory were encouraged to pray together, study together, and help each other.

The Oratory also placed a high value on joy and laughter. Neri believed that having a pleasant and positive attitude toward life was vital for spiritual development. He frequently used humor and narrative to express spiritual truths.

The Oratory had a profound impact on Rome. It evolved into a spiritual regeneration center as well as a source of hope and inspiration. The Oratory also participated in social and philanthropic activities, assisting the impoverished, sick, and marginalized.

The Oratory's success prompted the formation of new communities in other Italian cities and across Europe. The Oratory exerted a significant influence on the Catholic Church and society. It contributed to spiritual renewal, reform, and the growth of the Catholic faith.

The Oratory of Divine Love is a lively community today. It is a place where people can gather to pray, learn, and serve God in an atmosphere of joy, love, and camaraderie.

The Oratory's Unique Approach to Spirituality

Saint Philip Neri created the Oratory of Divine Love in Rome in 1551, and it is a unique lay community dedicated to spiritual rejuvenation and service. The Oratory's approach to spirituality is distinguished by its emphasis on joy, community, and reflection.

"The Emphasis is On Joy"

The Oratory's approach to spirituality is distinguished by its emphasis on joy. Neri believed that having a pleasant and positive attitude toward life was vital for spiritual development. He frequently used humor and narrative to express spiritual truths.

Neri's demeanor exemplified enthusiasm and positivity. He was recognized for his contagious laugh and ability to find humor in the most terrible situations. He thought that joy was a gift from God that should be nurtured and shared with others.

Spiritual practices in the oratory reflect the emphasis on joy. The members of the oratory were urged to pray with joy and appreciation. They were also taught to find joy in their daily lives, even in the face of obstacles and problems.

The Role of Community

The Oratory's approach to spirituality is also notable for its emphasis on community. Neri thought that spiritual development was best attained within a helpful and loving community.

The Oratory was a close-knit group that shared their lives and experiences. They prayed together, studied together, and helped each other in times of need.

The oratory's spiritual practices reflect its community-focused approach. Members of the Oratory were encouraged to pray together, share their joys and sorrows, and provide each other support on their spiritual journeys.

The Practice of Contemplation

In addition to joy and companionship, the oratory emphasized reflection. Neri felt that contemplation was necessary to deepen one's relationship with God.

The oratory's approach to contemplation was straightforward and pragmatic. Members of the Oratory were encouraged to engage in peaceful prayer and meditation. They were also encouraged to read the Bible and other spiritual writings.

The spiritual practices at the oratory reflect its emphasis on contemplation. Members of the Oratory were encouraged to engage in peaceful prayer and meditation. They were also encouraged to read the Bible and other spiritual writings.

The Oratory's approach to spirituality was radically different from the more austere and formal ways that were prevalent in the Catholic Church at the time. Neri's emphasis on joy, community, and contemplation contributed to a more inviting and inclusive atmosphere for individuals of all ages and backgrounds.

The Oratory's approach to spirituality remains relevant today. It provides a refreshing and inspirational alternative to the individualistic and consumer-driven approaches that are common in contemporary religions.

The Oratory's Impact on Rome

Saint Philip Neri created the Oratory of Divine Love in Rome in 1551, which had a great impact on the city and its inhabitants. The Oratory's significance is seen in its contributions to spiritual renewal, social change, and cultural life.

Spiritual Renewal

One of the most important ways the Oratory influenced Rome was through its commitment to spiritual rejuvenation. The oratory's emphasis on joy, community, and contemplation contributed to a more inviting and inclusive atmosphere for people of all ages and backgrounds.

The oratory's spiritual practices had a tremendous impact on the city's religious life. The Oratory's emphasis on prayer, study, and service motivated many people to grow in their spiritual lives.

The Oratory's influence on spiritual regeneration extended beyond Rome.

The Oratory's ideals and practices expanded throughout Italy and Europe, helping to reinvigorate the Catholic Church.

Social Reform

The Oratory also had an important influence on social reform. The oratory was dedicated to serving the impoverished, sick, and oppressed. The Oratory founded schools, hospitals, and other humanitarian organizations.

The Oratory's efforts in social change were driven by the concept that all persons are made in the image of God and that it is Christians' responsibility to care for one another. The Oratory's efforts to assist the destitute and needy improved the lives of many people in Rome.

Cultural Influence

The Oratory had a profound impact on Rome's cultural life. The oratory was a hub for intellectual and cultural activity. The Oratory's members included numerous scholars, artists, and musicians.

The Oratory's encouragement of the arts contributed to the development of new kinds of art and music. Many Renaissance artists and musicians have cited the Oratory as an influence in their work.

The Oratory had a tremendous impact on Rome. The Oratory's contributions to spiritual renewal, social reform, and cultural life aided Rome's revitalization and dynamic development. The Oratory's legacy can still be felt in Rome today.

The Oratory Spreads Throughout Europe

Saint Philip Neri created the Oratory of Divine Love in Rome in 1551, which had a major impact on the Catholic Church and European civilization. The Oratory's impact is seen in its contributions to spiritual renewal, reform, and the dissemination of the Catholic religion.

The Early Years

The Oratory's success in Rome prompted the formation of new communities in other towns in Italy and throughout Europe. The first oratory outside of Rome was established in Naples in 1564. Oratories were quickly erected in Florence, Venice, and other Italian cities.

Missionaries were sent to other regions to promote the oratory's ideas and practices, which aided its growth throughout Europe. These missionaries had an important role in exposing the oratory to new audiences and forming new communities.

The Oratory's spread into Europe was not without hurdles. Some members of the church hierarchy objected to the oratory's unconventional approach to spirituality. The Oratory also encountered financial difficulties and other practical issues.

Despite these limitations, the Oratory expanded and spread across Europe. By the end of the sixteenth century, oratories had been established in many major European towns, including Paris, Madrid, and Vienna.

The Oratory's Impact

The Oratory exerted a significant influence on the Catholic Church and European society. The Oratory's emphasis on joy, community, and contemplation contributed to a more inviting and inclusive atmosphere for people of all ages and backgrounds.

The Oratory's social reform efforts had a tremendous impact on European society. The Oratory's efforts to assist the impoverished, sick, and underprivileged served to improve many people's lives.

The Oratory's impact on the Catholic Church was likewise important. The Oratory's emphasis on spiritual renewal and reform helped to rejuvenate and strengthen the Church's position in Europe.

The Oratory's influence is seen in the numerous religious groups and congregations that were inspired by its example. The Oratory's effect can also be observed in the emergence of new kinds of Catholic spirituality and devotion.

The Oratory Today

The Oratory of Divine Love is a lively community today. There are oratories in numerous nations around the world. The Oratory's mission now is the same as it was in the sixteenth century: to foster spiritual renewal, to aid the poor and needy, and to propagate the Gospel.

The Oratory's approach to spirituality remains relevant today. The Oratory's emphasis on joy, community, and contemplation provides a welcome and inspirational contrast to the increasingly individualistic and consumer-driven methods that are common in contemporary spirituality.

Three

NERI'S EXTRAORDINARY GIFTS

The Gift of Laughter and Joy

One of the most notable elements of Saint Philip Neri's demeanor was his infectious laughter. This seemingly contradictory characteristic, together with his great spirituality, would become the defining feature of his life and career. Neri's laughter was more than a surface show of fun; it was a profound wellspring of delight stemming from his meeting with God.

Neri's chuckle was contagious. Those who knew him said his cheerful laugh could brighten even the darkest of days. His biographer, Bacci, describes how Neri's laughter would frequently fill the oratory, "like the sound of a bell ringing merrily." This infectious laughter was more than a personal quirk; it was a tremendous instrument that Neri utilized to bring others closer to God.

Neri believed that joy was a vital part of the spiritual life. He frequently emphasized the necessity of developing a sense of humor and finding joy in ordinary situations. In his sermons and conferences, he regularly used amusing anecdotes and parables to emphasize spiritual concepts. He felt that laughter could tear down boundaries, neutralize resistance, and open hearts to God's grace.

Neri's use of humor was neither frivolous nor rude. He took care to discern between laughing and ridicule, joy and disrespect. He believed that authentic humor was based on love and respect for others. He frequently utilized humor to illustrate human nature's foibles and hypocrisies, but always with a kind touch and a compassionate attitude.

Neri's laughter reflected his great faith and steadfast belief in God's benevolence. He felt that God was a kind and merciful Father who wished his children's happiness. He saw the world through the lens of God's love, and he faced life's trials and suffering with joy and optimism.

Neri's laughter was a poignant reminder of the gospel's transformational power. It demonstrated that even in the middle of life's tragedies and sorrows, one may find joy and serenity in God. His laughter served as a reminder that the spiritual life is not about gloomy seriousness or self-righteousness but rather about love, joy, and a deep connection with God.

The Gift of Healing and Miracles

In addition to his gift for humor, Saint Philip Neri was well-known for his exceptional ability to heal the sick and perform miracles. His reputation as a healer grew across Rome and beyond, and people from all walks of life sought his help.

Neri's healing miracles were frequently highly dramatic. There are several reports of him healing the blind, lame, and deaf. He was also renowned for his ability to revive the dead. One particularly vivid story is that of a small boy who drowned in the Tiber River. Neri prayed over the boy's body, and to the surprise of everyone present, the boy came back to life.

Neri's healing miracles were more than just acts of bodily regeneration; they were profound manifestations of God's mercy. He thought that healing was more than just medical knowledge or human intervention; it was a supernatural work of God requiring faith from both the healer and the healed.

Neri frequently stressed the role of faith in healing. He told his disciples that if they had the faith of a mustard seed, they could move mountains. He thought that true healing came from within, via a strong faith in God's power and love.

Neri's healing miracles were not isolated incidents; they were part of a broader process of spiritual rebirth and transformation. He believed that physical healing was frequently a prelude to spiritual recovery. He was not only healing people's bodies but also bringing them closer to God.

Neri's healing miracles demonstrated the power of God's love. They demonstrated that even in the midst of disease and suffering, God is present and active in the world. They served as a reminder that nothing is impossible with God and that his love can alter even the most seemingly hopeless situations.

The Gift of Discernment And Wisdom

Another of Saint Philip's unique abilities was his ability to read the minds and intentions of others. He was often referred to as having a "sixth sense" for reading people's hearts. This gift enabled him to provide insightful advice and spiritual direction to people who sought his assistance.

Neri's capacity to read people's thoughts and intents was more than just a psychological insight; it was a spiritual gift due to God's favor. He believed that God had given him the power to see beyond the surface of people's lives and into the depths of their spirits.

Neri used his talent of perception to help others on their spiritual journey. He was an expert confessor, and people from many walks of life sought him counsel on issues of religion and morals. He was noted for his ability to cut through people's excuses and rationalizations and get to the heart of their difficulties.

Neri's guidance was always based on love and compassion. He was never judgmental or critical; he always treated others with understanding and respect. He felt that everyone was capable of growth and change, and he frequently provided practical counsel and encouragement to assist others in overcoming their obstacles.

Neri's wisdom and practical advice stemmed from his extensive spiritual experience. He had a deep awareness of the human heart and the difficulties that people experience in their search for holiness. He was able to provide instruction that was both spiritual and practical.

Neri's gift of discernment served as a poignant reminder of the value of spiritual discernment in the Christian life. Discernment is the ability to tell the difference between good and evil, truth and lie. It is a valuable tool for negotiating the intricacies of the spiritual life.

Neri's example demonstrates that spiritual discernment is more than just an intellectual exercise; it is a matter of the heart. It involves humility, prayer, and readiness to hear God's voice within us. By practicing the skill of discernment, we can learn to negotiate our own life issues while also offering insight and support to others.

The Gift of Prophecy and Vision

Saint Philip Neri was well-known for his prophetic visions as well as his gifts of laughter, healing, and discernment. These visions were frequently supernatural occurrences in which Neri received messages or revelations from God. These visions were not always simple to comprehend, but they frequently guided and encouraged Neri and others around him.

Neri's prophetic visions were frequently highly spectacular. He would occasionally get visions of the future or events taking place far away. He also experienced visions of saints and angels. These visions were a source of great consolation and inspiration for Neri, and they encouraged him to strengthen his relationship with God.

Several of Neri's prophecies were fulfilled during his lifetime. For example, he anticipated Pope Pius IV's death and the election of Pope Pius V. He also foresaw the spread of the disease in Rome. These forecasts helped to develop Neri's reputation as a godly man, and they drew others to him for spiritual guidance.

For ages, people have debated the function of prophecy in the Church. Some Christians believe that prophecy is still alive today, while others believe it ended with the apostles' deaths. Regardless of one's beliefs about prophecy, it is obvious that it was crucial in the early Church.

Neri's prophetic visions emphasized the significance of spiritual discernment. Not all visions come from God; therefore, it is critical to be able to distinguish between authentic and false prophecies. Neri himself warned against the perils of false prophecy and asked his followers to be cautious in their approach to spiritual concerns.

Neri's visions served as a reminder of the importance of visions in the spiritual life. Visions are not just intellectual experiences; they are encounters with the Divine. They may provide enormous comfort, inspiration, and guidance.

Four

NERI'S RELATIONSHIP WITH THE CHURCH

Devotion to The Pope

Neri's steadfast devotion to the Pope was the foundation of his faith and ministry. He saw the Pope as the Vicar of Christ, the visible head of the Church, and held him in the highest regard. Neri's dedication to the Pope was more than just obedience; it was rooted in a genuine confidence in the holy institution of the papacy.

Neri's devotion to the Pope was clear in both his acts and writings. He consistently defended the Pope against his opponents, both within and outside of the Church. He backed the Pope's policies, even if they were unpopular or contentious. He pushed others to accept the Pope's authority and taught that dissent was a sin.

Neri's dedication to the Pope was neither blind nor unthinking. He was not afraid to express his opinion when he considered the Pope was mistaken. However, he always addressed the Pope with respect and humility, never questioning his authority.

Neri's devotion to the Pope was a significant part of his spiritual life. He felt that by praising the Pope, he was honoring Christ himself. He taught that obeying the Pope was a way to carry out the mandate to love one another.

Neri's dedication to the Pope was an integral part of his ministry. He utilized his position to support the Pope's authority and defend the Church's unity. He taught that the Church is one, holy, catholic, and apostolic, and that it is led by the Pope.

Neri's devotion to the Pope was a source of strength and inspiration for many Catholics in the 16th century. His example helped to build church unity and reinforce the papacy's relevance.

Role in Church Reforms

Neri played a diverse and crucial part in the sixteenth-century church reforms. He was a spiritual reformer, an advocate for Catholic education, and an opponent of heresy and schism. His impact extended throughout the Church, and his memory continues to inspire Catholics today.

Neri was a spiritual reformer, in the best meaning of the term. He was strongly committed to the rebirth of the Church and fought relentlessly to restore the purity and simplicity of the early Church. He was especially worried with the spiritual degradation that occurred in the church throughout the fifteenth and sixteenth centuries. He felt that the church should return to its roots, find its original mission, and reclaim its spiritual power.

Neri's Oratory of Divine Love was an important part of his spiritual rehabilitation. The Oratory was a lay society that welcomed both priests and laymen. Its members were bound together by a common desire for spiritual growth, intellectual advancement, and charitable service. The oratory exemplified a new type of religious life based on community, simplicity, and active participation in the world.

Neri was also an advocate of Catholic education. He believed that education was critical to the rebirth of the church. He established various schools and seminaries, and he encouraged his followers to seek academic and spiritual development. Neri's emphasis on education helped to revive the Church's intellectual life while also training a new generation of dedicated priests and laity.

Neri was an opponent of heresy and schism. He was greatly concerned about the Protestant Reformation and its threat to the Church's unity. He strove to preserve the Catholic religion against Protestant attacks, and he urged Catholics to be faithful to the Pope and Church. Neri's efforts contributed to fortifying the Catholic Church's position during the Counter-Reformation.

Neri left a great imprint in the sixteenth-century church reforms. He was a spiritual reformer, an advocate for Catholic education, and an opponent of heresy and schism. His impact extended throughout the Church, and his memory continues to inspire Catholics today.

Influence on Counter-Reformation

Neri's impact on the Counter-Reformation was significant and far-reaching. His emphasis on joy, simplicity, and fellowship influenced Catholics' devotional practices at the time. His Oratory of Divine Love served as a model for new religious communities, and his ideas on spiritual rejuvenation influenced many people.

Neri's emphasis on joy represented a fundamental break from the religious climate of the sixteenth century. The Counter-Reformation was a period of enormous spiritual and social upheaval, and many Catholics felt profound shame and sorrow. Neri's message of joy and hope was refreshing. He taught us that God loved us unconditionally and that we were meant to live lives of joy and appreciation. Neri's emphasis on pleasure contributed to a more pleasant and welcoming atmosphere in the Catholic Church.

Neri's insistence on simplicity contributed significantly to his effect on the Counter-Reformation. He believed that the actual route to holiness lay in the simplest aspects of life. He encouraged his followers to avoid worldly distractions and concentrate on the core principles of the Christian faith. Neri's insistence on simplicity helped to purify the Catholic Church and restore it to its roots.

Neri's emphasis on community had a great impact on the Counter-Reformation. He believed that the Christian life was most effectively lived in community with others. He established the Oratory of Divine Love, a lay society focused on the values of fraternity, compassion, and mutual assistance. The Oratory was a model for new religious communities and helped to rejuvenate the Catholic Church's social life.

Neri's ideas on spiritual regeneration also had a significant impact on the Counter-Reformation. He taught that spiritual rebirth could not be accomplished through exterior actions alone. Rather, it required a profound alteration of the heart and mind. Neri's emphasis on spiritual renewal encouraged Catholics to seek a closer relationship with God and live their lives in conformity with the Gospel.

Neri's impact on the Counter-Reformation was significant and far-reaching.

His emphasis on joy, simplicity, and fellowship influenced Catholics' devotional practices at the time. His Oratory of Divine Love served as a model for new religious communities, and his ideas on spiritual rejuvenation influenced many people. Neri's legacy can still be felt in the Catholic Church today.

Legacy Within The Church

Neri's influence in the Catholic Church is enormous and lasting. He is revered as the patron saint of Rome, comedians, and people seeking a joyous spiritual life. His Oratory of Divine Love remains a thriving community, and his ideas on spiritual renewal continue to inspire Catholics today.

Pope Gregory XV canonized Neri in 1622. He was given the title "Apostle of Rome" in appreciation of his contributions to the city's spiritual rebirth. Neri is also known as the patron saint of comedians due to his infectious laugh and ability to utilize comedy to express spiritual truths. He is also the patron saint of those who desire a joyful spiritual life.

Neri built the Oratory of Divine Love, which remains a flourishing community today. The Oratory is a lay community that welcomes both priests and laity. Its members are bound together by a common desire for spiritual growth, intellectual advancement, and charitable service. The Oratory has expanded throughout the world and continues to provide spiritual renewal and inspiration.

Neri's ideas on spiritual rejuvenation are pertinent today. He taught that spiritual rebirth could not be accomplished through exterior actions alone. Rather, it required a profound alteration of the heart and mind. Neri's emphasis on joy, simplicity, and community remains relevant today. In a society that is frequently fast-paced, materialistic, and individualistic, Neri's message of joy, simplicity, and community can be both comforting and inspiring.

Neri's influence in the Catholic Church is enormous and lasting. He is revered as the patron saint of Rome, comedians, and people seeking a joyous spiritual life. His Oratory of Divine Love remains a thriving community, and his ideas on spiritual renewal continue to inspire Catholics today.

Five

NERI'S SPIRITUAL TEACHINGS

The Importance of Joy and Laughter

Joy and laughter appear as colorful threads in the tapestry of Saint Philip Neri's spiritual teachings, which are weaved with a unique blend of knowledge, humor, and irresistible passion. Neri's life was a shining example of these traits, blazing the path to holiness with her captivating smile and joyful laugh. He believed that joy and laughter were not frivolous diversions but rather fundamental components of a healthy and spiritual existence, a gift from God to be received and shared with the world.

Neri's understanding of joy was everything but shallow. He saw it as a profound statement of thankfulness, acknowledging God's generosity and love in our lives. Joy, he believed, was a potent antidote to the sadness and sorrow that so often plague the human heart. It provided strength, resilience, and optimism in the face of hardship.

Neri approached spirituality with a refreshing sense of humor. He was an excellent storyteller, utilizing anecdotes, jokes, and humorous observations to express profound spiritual truths. He thought that laughter could break down barriers, lift spirits, and bring people closer together. Humor, he frequently stated, was a gift from God, a chance to connect with others on a deeper level and share the joy of Christ.

Neri's infectious laughter was a distinguishing feature of his personality. It was a contagious sound, and his joyous countenance seemed to brighten every room he visited. His laughing was more than just a surface statement of amusement; it was a deep-seated delight that flowed from within. It was a reflection of his love for God and his fellow humans, as well as a representation of the serenity and contentment he had discovered through his relationship with Christ.

Neri's belief in the power of joy and laughter was founded on his own personal experience. He had faced adversity and pain in his life, but he had also witnessed the transformational power of joy. He had learned that even at the darkest moments, there was always a reason to grin, a ray of light that could cut through the fog.

Neri's teachings about joy and laughter have inspired and influenced people for millennia. His legacy serves as a reminder that spirituality is more about joy, love, and a deep connection with God than seriousness and solemnity. It is a call to live life with a sense of humor, thankfulness, and hope, and to spread that joy throughout the world.

The Practice of Simplicity and Humility

In the rich tapestry of Saint Philip Neri's spiritual teachings, the virtues of simplicity and humility emerge as threads of enduring knowledge, woven with quiet strength and a deep awareness of the human heart. Neri, a man of humble origins and deep faith, understood the perils of materialism and the value of living a simple and unpretentious life. He felt that true happiness might be found in cultivating a simple and contented heart rather than in material riches or worldly success.

Neri preached against materialism, the chase of wealth and possessions that can lead us astray from the genuine meaning of life. He saw materialism as a hindrance to spiritual development, a source of dissatisfaction and misery. Instead, he advised his followers to live a simple life, focusing on the necessities and giving up needless belongings.

Neri's lessons on simplicity did not involve deprivation or asceticism. He thought that a simple existence was one free of clutter and distractions, allowing us to concentrate on what is truly important. He taught his followers to live within their means, avoid debt, and be generous to those in need.

Neri also highlighted the value of humility, acknowledging one's own limits, and relying on God. He believed that humility was necessary for spiritual development, healthy interpersonal connections, and leading a life of service.

Neri's humility did not involve self-deprecation or phony modesty. It was a true recognition of his own limits combined with a sincere faith in God's providence. He was a man of profound humility but also of immense confidence and courage. He understood that his power came from God, not from himself, and he was willing to rely on God's grace in whatever he did.

Neri's teachings on simplicity and humility have continued to inspire and impact people for ages. His legacy serves as a reminder that true happiness is found in cultivating a simple and pleased heart rather than in material possessions or worldly achievement. It is a call to live a humble life, to acknowledge our own limits, and to trust in God's providence.

The Role of Community and Fellowship

In the rich tapestry of Saint Philip Neri's spiritual teachings, the necessity of community and fellowship emerges as a thread of enduring wisdom, woven with a deep awareness of the human heart and a strong belief in shared experiences. Neri, a guy with great social charisma and genuine compassion for his fellow humans, understood the critical role that community plays in our spiritual growth and development. He felt that we were not supposed to live alone but rather in community, and that our relationships with one another may help us better comprehend God and ourselves.

Neri's Oratory of Divine Love was an essential component of his spiritual vision. It was a community of Christians bound together by their common faith and dedication to spiritual advancement. The Oratory provided a venue for its members to gather in prayer, study, and friendship, to encourage one another on their spiritual journeys, and to see the transformational power of shared experiences.

Neri felt that shared experiences might strengthen our bonds with God and one another. He encouraged his followers to take an active role in the life of the oratory, to seek out chances for fellowship with other Christians, and to engage in activities that build a sense of community and belonging.

Neri's teachings on community and fellowship were not limited to social events or networking. They aimed to develop relationships based on love, respect, and mutual support. He believed that true community was defined by a sense of solidarity, compassion, and common purpose.

Neri's legacy emphasizes the value of community and camaraderie in our spiritual lives. It is a call to seek out opportunities for connection with people, to create strong bonds based on love and respect, and to witness the transformational power of shared experiences.

The Path of Spiritual Growth

In the rich tapestry of Saint Philip Neri's spiritual teachings, the way to spiritual growth emerges as a thread of enduring knowledge, woven with a deep awareness of the human heart and a great faith in God's transformative power. Neri, a man of tremendous spiritual insight and a lifelong search for truth, understood that spiritual progress was a lifetime process that required perseverance, discipline, and a strong dedication to God.

Neri believed that prayer was necessary to spiritual development. He encouraged his followers to pray on a regular basis, seek God's guidance and wisdom, and develop a personal relationship with him. Neri's prayer life was marked by sincere devotion and naive faith in God. Prayer, he believed, was more than just a religious responsibility; it was a source of strength, consolation, and inspiration.

Neri also stressed the significance of studying the Bible. He felt that the Scriptures provided inspiration, guidance, and knowledge. He encouraged his followers to study the Bible on a regular basis, reflect on its lessons, and apply them to their own lives.

Neri understood that spiritual growth necessitated self-discipline and a dedication to personal development. He pushed his disciples to exercise self-control, avoid temptation, and strive for excellence in everything they did. Neri was a man of exceptional discipline and self-control. He was recognized for his consistent habits, timeliness, and dedication to his spiritual practices.

Neri also thought that spiritual development was a process that required perseverance and patience. He acknowledged that there would be problems and disappointments along the way, but he encouraged his followers to keep their faith, trust in God's plan, and never give up on their spiritual journey.

Neri's legacy serves as a reminder that spiritual development is a lifetime process that requires effort, discipline, and a strong dedication to God. It is an invitation to seek out opportunities for spiritual growth, to develop a personal relationship with God through prayer and study, and to strive for excellence in all that we do.

Six

NERI'S IMPACT ON SOCIETY

Care for the Poor and Needy

St. Philip Neri's unrelenting compassion for the poor and destitute was a defining feature of his ministry. He believed that aiding the downtrodden was both a religious duty and a physical demonstration of God's love. Neri's Oratory became a haven for the needy, providing food, shelter, and spiritual instruction.

One of the oratory's most significant achievements was the installation of a soup kitchen, which served daily meals to the hungry. The soup kitchen was available to everyone, regardless of faith or social class. Neri frequently joined the volunteers in serving the meals, offering an example of humility and kindness.

Neri also made a point of visiting the sick and dying at their houses. He would bring them communion, offer words of comfort, and pray beside them. His presence brought immense comfort to those who were suffering, and his accounts of miracles and healings instilled hope and faith.

In addition to giving financial assistance, Neri fought for social justice and changes to address the underlying causes of poverty. He chastised the wealthy for their apathy to the plight of the poor and encouraged the government to take action to establish a more equitable society.

Neri's dedication to the poor and needy sprang from his strong faith and belief in the intrinsic dignity of all humans. He saw God's image in every person, no matter how humble or outcast. His kindness and generosity inspired his contemporaries and still serve as a model for Christians today.

Promoting Education and Culture

St. Philip Neri was a fervent supporter of education and culture, thinking that they were necessary for the spiritual and intellectual development of persons and societies. He understood that education was a strong instrument for uplifting the poor and underprivileged, and he was dedicated to providing educational opportunities to all.

One of Neri's most notable contributions to education was the construction of a school within the oratory. The school welcomed boys from all social backgrounds and provided a challenging curriculum that emphasized both academic topics and spiritual development. Neri took a considerable interest in the boys' education, frequently visiting their classes and offering advice and support.

Neri also promoted the work of artists and scholars, emphasizing the value of culture in improving the human experience. He encouraged his Oratorians to pursue intellectual interests and frequently organized literary and musical events at the Oratory. Neri's sponsorship of the arts contributed to Rome's strong cultural atmosphere, and his impact may still be felt today in the city's artistic traditions.

Neri's commitment to education and culture sprang from his belief in the dignity of the human being. He saw education as a way to enable people to attain their greatest potential and contribute to the advancement of society. His influence in this area is still being acknowledged today, and his oratory serves as a center for study and culture.

Influence on Art and Literature

St. Philip Neri's influence stretched far beyond the walls of his oratory, touching the lives of countless people via his passion for music, literature, and the arts. His enthusiasm for these disciplines was contagious, pushing people to pursue their own creative interests and use their gifts to praise God.

Neri adored music, especially holy music and choral singing. He thought that music had the ability to boost the spirit and draw people closer to God. Neri frequently led the singing in the oratory, and he encouraged his oratorians to participate in the church's musical activities. His encouragement of music contributed to Rome's vibrant musical legacy, and his influence may still be heard in the city's churches today.

Neri also had a strong passion for literature and was noted for his ability to relate stories in a colorful and captivating way. His homilies and sermons were frequently interspersed with tales, parables, and funny illustrations, which his audience anxiously anticipated. Neri's influence on Italian literature is evident in the works of various writers who were inspired by his example.

In addition to his passion for music and literature, Neri supported the arts in other ways. He encouraged his orators to pursue artistic activities and frequently held events with painters, sculptors, and other artists. Neri's sponsorship of the arts contributed to Rome's thriving cultural landscape, and his legacy may still be seen today.

St. Philip Neri's influence on the arts and literature reflected his belief in the ability of beauty and creativity to improve the human experience. He saw art as a way to communicate God's glory and encourage people to live more fully. His influence in this field is still acknowledged today, and his oratory serves as a hub for artistic expression and innovation.

Legacy of Rome and Beyond

St. Philip Neri's legacy in Rome and beyond demonstrates the persistent strength of his vision and the lasting impact of his ministry. His oratory remains a thriving hub of spiritual and cultural activity, and his teachings continue to inspire people all over the world.

The Oratory of Divine Love in Rome continues to bear witness to Neri's legacy. Carlo Maderno, a renowned architect, designed the church, which is a Baroque masterpiece. The Oratory community maintains Neri's purpose of spiritual rejuvenation and assistance to the impoverished, and it is still a famous pilgrimage and tourist site.

Neri's impact spread far beyond Rome, with the Oratory establishing colonies in various towns across Italy and Europe. These communities embraced Neri's spirituality and commitment to social justice, and they contributed significantly to the Catholic revival of the 16th and seventeenth centuries.

Neri's legacy had a significant impact on the Catholic Church as a whole. His emphasis on joy, simplicity, and community helped to revive the church following the Reformation. His example influenced countless priests and religious to pursue more active and involved ministries, and his teachings are still relevant to the Church today.

St. Philip's legacy in Rome and beyond exemplifies the enduring power of faith, hope, and love. His life and efforts continue to inspire people of all ages and backgrounds, and his oratory still shines brightly in the heart of the Eternal City.

Seven

NERI'S DEATH AND LEGACY

The Circumstances of His Death

Saint Philip Neri's life, marked by exceptional events and spiritual encounters, came to an end in the early hours of May 26, 1595. Neri's health deteriorated in his latter years. The demands of his ministry, along with his old age, had taken a toll on his physical stamina. Despite his failing health, Neri continued to carry out his duties with unabated passion, visiting the ill, preaching, and providing spiritual assistance to those in need.

Neri's condition worsened, and he became more aware of his impending death. He confronted his mortality with peace and acceptance, trusting in God's will. In the days before his death, Neri gathered his spiritual children around him, offering them words of encouragement and farewell. He exhorted them to maintain their faith and continue the oratory's work.

On the evening of May 25, Neri retired to his bed, his body exhausted from illness. As the night progressed, his breathing got difficult and his pulse became weak. Those gathered around his bedside watched with sorrow and expectation, their hearts heavy with the realization that their beloved spiritual father was nearing the end of his earthly life.

Finally, in the early hours of May 26, Saint Philip Neri passed away quietly. His death was a source of great sadness and loss for the Oratory and the entire city of Rome. However, it was also a time of joy for Neri's devoted disciples, who delighted in the knowledge that their beloved saint had entered eternal life.

Neri's death was an appropriate conclusion to a life defined by exceptional sanctity and unswerving commitment to God. He had led a life of simplicity, humility, and unselfish devotion, encouraging many people to follow in his footsteps. His legacy would live on, demonstrating the power of faith, hope, and love.

The Canonization Process

The canonization of Saint Philip Neri was a lengthy and intricate procedure that took several decades. It entailed a thorough examination of his life, virtues, and miracles, ending in a papal declaration proclaiming him a saint.

The first step in the canonization process was gathering evidence to support Neri's case. This included testimony from individuals who knew Jesus during his lifetime, as well as evidence of his miracles and other exceptional actions. The Oratory of Divine Love, created by Neri, was instrumental in gathering and preserving this evidence.

The evidence was collected and submitted to the Congregation for the Causes of Saints, a Vatican agency in charge of overseeing the canonization process.

The Congregation established a special tribunal to probe Neri's life and activity. The tribunal thoroughly studied the material, interviewing witnesses and specialists before concluding that Neri led an exemplary life of holiness.

The next step in the procedure was to beatify Neri. The Pope made an official pronouncement that Neri was a servant of God. Beatification is usually the first step toward canonization and permits the public worship of the saint's relics.

In 1605, Pope Clement VIII beatified Saint Philip Neri. This was a big step forward in the canonization process, although Neri was not yet declared a saint. To be canonized, a saint must have performed a second miracle after death.

It was several years before a second miracle was attributed to Saint Philip Neri. Finally, in 1622, Pope Gregory XV made Neri a saint. The papal decree acknowledged Neri's exceptional qualities and forceful intercession on behalf of the believers.

Saint Philip Neri's canonization was a success for the Oratory and a monument to his extraordinary legacy. The Catholic Church officially recognized Neri's sanctity, paving the path for his devotion around the world.

The Spread of His Devotion

Following his canonization in 1622, devotion to Saint Philip Neri expanded far beyond Rome. The Oratory of Divine Love, which Neri created, spread to other places in Italy and abroad. Neri's captivating demeanor, along with his practical approach to spirituality, appealed to individuals of all ages and backgrounds.

NERI'S DEATH AND LEGACY

The oratory's aim was to foster spiritual rejuvenation while also providing a haven of sanctuary and camaraderie for the faithful. The Oratorians emphasized the value of community, intellectual growth, and service to the needy. Their emphasis on joy and laughter distinguished them from other religious organizations, resulting in a diverse and enthusiastic following.

Neri's writings and teachings also played an important part in promoting his faith. His publications, which included letters, sermons, and spiritual exercises, were well-read and translated into other languages. Neri's emphasis on simplicity, humility, and a sense of humor made his writings accessible to readers of all educational levels.

The worship of Saint Philip's relics also helped to strengthen his devotion. Neri was initially buried in Rome's Oratory of Divine Love. In 1613, his remains were moved to a new church dedicated to him. The church, called the Chiesa del Gesù e San Filippo Neri, immediately became a renowned pilgrimage destination.

Pilgrims from all over the world visited the church to revere Neri's relics and seek his intervention. The power of Neri's relics was widely believed, and his intervention was credited with many miraculous healings and other supernatural events.

The expansion of Saint Philip Neri's devotion demonstrated the continuing attraction of his message. His emphasis on joy, holiness, and community appealed to individuals of all ages and ethnicities. Neri built the Oratory of Divine Love, which is still a dynamic and active community today, carrying on his legacy of spiritual renewal and service to the impoverished.

The Effect of His Life on the World

Saint Philip Neri's life and legacy had a great impact on the Catholic Church and the wider world. His beliefs and example have impacted numerous people, demonstrating his influence.

Neri's emphasis on joy and laughter marked a significant break from the spiritual milieu of his time. In an age of religious austerity and moral rigidity, Neri's message was refreshing change. He demonstrated that holiness might be discovered in everyday moments, in the modest pleasures of human existence.

Neri's Oratory of Divine Love had a tremendous influence on the Catholic Church. The Oratory's emphasis on community, intellectual development, and charitable work inspired subsequent religious groups. The oratory's success in attracting and maintaining members indicated that a more adaptive approach to religious life was feasible.

Neri's legacy is most obvious in Rome, where he lived and ministered. The Oratory of Divine Love, located in the heart of the city, is still a thriving and active community. Neri's tomb in the Chiesa del Gesù e San Filippo Neri is a famous pilgrimage destination. The saint's image can be found around the city as a reminder of his eternal presence.

Neri's influence stretches well beyond Rome and the Catholic Church. His ideas on joy, sanctity, and community have appealed to individuals of various ages and backgrounds. His example has encouraged many others to pursue a deeper spiritual life and make a positive change in the world.

Saint Philip Neri's continuing popularity stems from his ability to connect with others on a human level. His warmth, humor, and compassion made him a popular figure throughout his lifetime, and his legacy continues to inspire and encourage people today. Neri's message is timeless, reminding us that joy, sanctity, and love are necessary ingredients for a successful and meaningful life.

Eight

ST. PHILIP NERI TODAY

The Relevance of His Teachings

Saint Philip Neri, often known as the "Apostle of Rome," was a man of great joy, sanctity, and spiritual depth. His life and teachings continue to motivate and impact individuals of all ages and origins. One of the most enduring features of Neri's legacy is his focus on the value of joy and laughter in spiritual practice.

In a world rife with tension, anxiety, and a sense of overpowering darkness, Neri's lessons on joy provide a welcome and much-needed respite. He believed that laughter was not only a natural and healthy human expression but also an effective tool for spiritual development. Neri frequently used humor and storytelling to express great spiritual principles, making his teachings understandable and entertaining to people of all ages and ethnicities.

Neri's emphasis on joy did not represent a shallow or frivolous attitude toward spirituality. Rather, it was founded on a thorough grasp of the nature of God and the human spirit. He believed that God is the source of endless love and contentment and that our ultimate fulfillment is found in union with Him. By nurturing an attitude of joy and appreciation, we can connect with God's will and live to the fullest.

Neri's teachings on joy are especially timely in today's environment, where many individuals are dealing with depression, anxiety, and other mental health difficulties. By adopting a joyful mindset, we can increase our resilience, better cope with life's obstacles, and nurture a sense of calm and well-being.

In addition to joy, Neri highlighted the value of simplicity and humility. He felt that these virtues were necessary for spiritual development and might be fostered via a life of prayer, meditation, and service to others. Neri led a humble and quiet life, eschewing earthly possessions in favor of those that would bring him closer to God.

Neri's teachings on simplicity and humility are especially timely in today's consumer-driven culture, where many individuals are tempted to identify themselves based on their things and achievements. By adopting a simpler lifestyle, we can liberate ourselves from the shackles of materialism and focus on what is truly important in life.

Neri's teachings also emphasized the value of community and fellowship. He thought that we were not created to live alone but rather in community with others. Neri established the Oratory of Divine Love, a lay community dedicated to spiritual development and service to the underprivileged. The oratory became a model for the supporting and loving community that Neri believed was necessary for spiritual growth.

Neri's teachings about community and fellowship are especially pertinent in today's environment, where many people feel lonely and disconnected from others. Building meaningful relationships with others allows us to gain support, encouragement, and a sense of belonging.

Finally, Neri's teachings provide advice on the road of spiritual development. He felt that spiritual growth was a lifelong process that required perseverance, discipline, and a readiness to accept God's favor. Neri encouraged his disciples to seek spiritual guidance, practice frequent prayer and meditation, and live a life of service to others.

Neri's lessons on spiritual growth are especially pertinent now, when many people are looking for meaning and purpose in their lives. By following Neri's advice, we can go on a spiritual path of discovery and transformation.

In conclusion, Saint Philip Neri's lessons on joy, simplicity, humility, community, and spiritual growth remain relevant and encouraging in today's world. By following these lessons, we can build a greater sense of joy, peace, and contentment in our lives.

Oratory in the Modern World

Saint Philip Neri created the Oratory of Divine Love in the sixteenth century, and it remains a dynamic and significant community in the Catholic Church today. The oratory's purpose is to foster spiritual and intellectual development, as well as communal service. Today, the Oratory has a global presence, with groups in several countries across the world.

One of the most significant issues facing the oratory in the modern era is the necessity to adjust its mission and practices to fit the changing requirements of contemporary society. In recent years, the Oratory has emphasized problems such as poverty, homelessness, and environmental damage. In addition, the oratory promotes interfaith communication and understanding, as well as a culture of peace and healing.

Despite the obstacles of the modern world, the oratory is a source of spiritual refreshment and progress. The oratory's members are dedicated to a life of prayer, study, and service. They are also encouraged to explore their intellectual and artistic abilities.

The oratory's spirituality emphasizes joy, camaraderie, and intellectual engagement. Members of the Oratory are urged to lead a balanced life that includes spiritual practices, intellectual interests, and social participation.

The Oratory's global presence has enabled it to reach a larger audience and have a profound impact on the world. Oratory communities can be found across Europe, North America, South America, Africa, and Asia. These communities allow people from various walks of life to come together for prayer, learning, and service.

The Oratory's dedication to social justice and interfaith communication is another significant component of its goal. The oratory promotes peace and reconciliation while addressing the core causes of poverty and injustice. The Oratory also aims to foster connections between individuals of many faiths and cultures.

Finally, the Oratory of Divine Love remains a thriving and prominent group inside the Catholic Church. The oratory's purpose is to foster spiritual and intellectual development, as well as communal service. The Oratory contributes significantly to the globe through its global presence, commitment to social justice, and interfaith engagement.

The oratory's spirituality emphasizes joy, camaraderie, and intellectual engagement. Members of the Oratory are urged to lead a balanced life that includes spiritual practices, intellectual interests, and social participation.

The Oratory's global presence has enabled it to reach a larger audience and have a profound impact on the world. Oratory communities can be found across Europe, North America, South America, Africa, and Asia. These communities allow people from various walks of life to come together for prayer, learning, and service.

The Oratory's dedication to social justice and interfaith communication is another significant component of its goal. The oratory promotes peace and reconciliation while addressing the core causes of poverty and injustice. The Oratory also aims to foster connections between individuals of many faiths and cultures.

Finally, the Oratory of Divine Love remains a thriving and prominent group inside the Catholic Church. The oratory's purpose is to foster spiritual and intellectual development, as well as communal service. The Oratory contributes significantly to the globe through its global presence, commitment to social justice, and interfaith engagement.

The Devotion to St. Philip Neri

Saint Philip Neri's life and teachings have inspired many people over the centuries. His devotion has extended well beyond the Catholic Church, and he is revered by people of various faiths and ethnicities.

Saint Philip's continued popularity can be attributed to his infectious joy and sense of humor. Neri's capacity to find joy in the midst of pain and adversity is a tremendous example for all of us. His laughter and tales have comforted and inspired countless people.

Saint Philip's renown stems in part from his deep spirituality. Neri was a man of deep faith who lived a life of meditation and reflection. His love for God was clear in everything he did, from his interactions with others to his work for the destitute.

Neri's legacy is also visible in the Oratory of Divine Love, the community he established. The Oratory remains a lively and prominent institution in the Catholic Church, demonstrating Neri's lasting legacy.

The devotion to Saint Philip Neri has been shown in different genres of art, literature, and music. His life has been the topic of several books, films, and artworks. Many Catholic churches and residences include a picture of Saint Philip Neri with a joyous look and outstretched arms.

The devotion to Saint Philip Neri has also had a great influence on popular culture. Neri's life and beliefs have been mentioned in numerous works of fiction, including novels, plays, and films. His name has also served as an inspiration to musicians, artists, and other creative folks.

Saint Philip Neri has recently gained popularity, particularly among young people. Neri's message of joy, hope, and compassion resonates with many people today, and his life serves as a great example of how to live a meaningful and fulfilled life.

The devotion to Saint Philip Neri reflects the ongoing strength of his legacy. His life and teachings continue to motivate and impact individuals of all ages and origins. Whether you are a devout Catholic or just looking for meaning and purpose in your life, Saint Philip Neri provides an inspiring example of how to live a joyful, holy, and purposeful life.

The Saint Who Continues To Inspire

Saint Philip Neri's life and teachings continue to motivate and impact individuals of all ages and backgrounds. His legacy demonstrates the enduring power of joy, sanctity, and compassion.

Neri's example is especially important in today's environment, which is typically marked by tension, anxiety, and a lack of hope. Neri's contagious pleasure and happiness are an effective antidote to the pessimism and sorrow that may quickly overwhelm us.

Neri's dedication to social justice and service to the disadvantaged is another facet of his legacy that continues to motivate. His life serves as a reminder that true spirituality entails more than simply personal devotion; it also includes caring for others and working for a more just and equitable world.

Neri's teachings on the value of community and fellowship are especially pertinent in today's environment, which can feel lonely and individualistic. Neri's Oratory of Divine Love exemplified the type of helpful and nurturing society required for spiritual growth and well-being.

Neri's life and teachings provide a compelling example of how to live a happy and fulfilling life. Despite the difficulties he encountered, Neri was always able to find joy and hope in his life. His example serves as a reminder that happiness is not derived from outward circumstances but rather from an inner attitude of thankfulness and satisfaction.

The devotion to Saint Philip Neri reflects the ongoing strength of his legacy. His life and teachings continue to motivate and impact individuals of all ages and origins. Whether you are a devout Catholic or just looking for meaning and purpose in your life, Saint Philip Neri provides an inspiring example of how to live a joyful, holy, and purposeful life.

Finally, Saint Philip's legacy serves as a reminder that joy, sanctity, and compassion can be lived even in the face of adversity. His example inspires individuals of many faiths and backgrounds, and his lessons remain relevant and valuable in today's world.

Nine

CONCLUSION

The Enduring Legacy of St. Philip Neri

The life and work of Saint Philip Neri demonstrate the enduring power of joy, purity, and a deep love for God and humanity. His tale, which is frequently eclipsed by more well-known people in the Catholic Church, provides a unique viewpoint on spiritual life and the transformational power of humanity.

Neri's legacy is varied. He is regarded as a spiritual giant, with a profound grasp of the human heart and an extraordinary ability to connect with people from all walks of life. His oratory, a community of secular clerics dedicated to spiritual regeneration, set a precedent for religious life in the sixteenth century and continues to inspire countless people today.

Neri's teachings about joy and laughter are especially notable. In a world filled with evil, pain, and despair, his message provides a welcome contrast.

He emphasizes that joy is more than just a passing emotion but rather a deep-rooted spiritual virtue that may sustain us even in the face of tragedy.

Neri's emphasis on community and camaraderie is equally significant. In an era of growing individuality and alienation, his vision of a church really united in love and service provides a compelling antidote. He emphasizes how our spiritual progress is closely related to our connections with others.

Neri's life exemplifies the transformational power of love. His unfailing compassion for the poor, sick, and oppressed was a defining feature of his ministry. He illustrated that true love is more than just a sentiment; it is a specific deed that includes self-sacrifice, generosity, and a willingness to serve others.

Neri's legacy reaches well beyond his own lifetime. His teachings and lifestyle continue to motivate people around the world. He founded the Oratory, which is still a flourishing community of spiritual seekers today. His feast day is honored by many Catholics, and his image may be found in churches and homes all around the world.

In conclusion, Saint Philip Neri's life and ministry convey a timeless message of hope, joy, and love. His narrative demonstrates that even in the darkest of circumstances, there is always room for light and hope. His legacy demonstrates the enduring power of the human spirit and the transformational possibilities of faith. As we reflect on his life and teachings, we are encouraged to seek a deeper connection with God and to live more fully in the present moment.

Made in the USA
Coppell, TX
12 April 2025